1293

917.64   Stewart, Gail
STE
          Houston

$14.60

DATE			
SEP 2 9 1992			

917.64
STE
Houston

1293

Houston

★ GREAT ★ CITIES ★ OF THE ★ USA ★

☆ ☆ ☆

LIBRARY OF CONGRESS CATALOGING-IN-PUBLICATION DATA
Stewart, Gail, 1949-
    Houston / by Gail B. Stewart.
        p. cm. -- (Great Cities of the United States)
    Summary: An introduction to the history, economy, people, and notable sites of
the largest city in Texas.
    ISBN 0-86592-539-9
    1. Houston (Tex.)--Description--1981- --Guide-books--Juvenile literature. [1.
Houston (Tex.)--Description--Guides.] I. Title. II. Series: Stewart, Gail, 1949-
Great Cities of the United States.
F394.H83S74 1989
917.64'14110463--dc20   89-32410
                                                                                         CIP
                                                                                         AC

☆ ☆ ☆

Houston

★ GREAT ★ CITIES ★ OF THE ★ USA ★

TEXT BY
GAIL STEWART

DESIGN & PRODUCTION BY
MARK E. AHLSTROM
(The Bookworks)

**ROURKE
ENTERPRISES,
INC.**
Vero Beach, FL 32964
U.S.A.

The
Bayou City...

☆ ☆ ☆

TABLE OF CONTENTS

CREDITS

All Photos: The Stockhouse, Inc., Houston, Texas

Scott Berner ....cover photo, 4, 6, 9, 21, ...22, 25, 27, 29, 30, 33, 38
R. Reagan Atkinson 7
Rick Stockton 10
James Ellenburg 11
John Patton 12
Roger A. Lloyd, Jr. 14-15
E. Lynn Baldwin 16, 31
W. C. Ging 17

Murray Getz 18-19
Michael Meyer 28
Jim Caldwell 32
Jim McNee 35, 36
Ben Smusz 37
S. J. Brown 39
Norman Lanier 41
Dale Kirksey 43

TYPESETTING AND LAYOUT: THE FINAL WORD
PRINTING: WORZALLA PUBLISHING CO.

★ ★ ☆

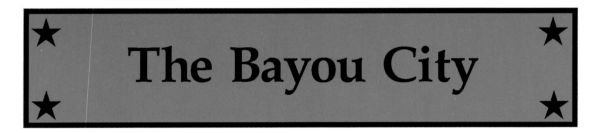
Every large city seems to have something that sets it apart from other places. It may be a reputation for great restaurants, or beautiful buildings. It might be the kind of industries for which that city is famous, or the quality of its theaters and museums.

People who live in Houston, Texas, are proud of their city because it has many characteristics that set it apart from other American cities. Called the Bayou City because of the swampy Buffalo Bayou that runs through it, Houston boasts museums, ballet, and theater. Its

The Johnson Space Center, located about 20 miles southeast of Houston, is the command post for every manned U.S. space flight and the training site for U.S. astronauts.

architecture is first-rate, and many of its restaurants—especially those specializing in Mexican food—are quite famous. But there is one thing that Houston can boast about that no other city can.

On July 20, 1969, astronauts Neil Armstrong and Edwin Aldrin landed on the moon. Armstrong told the space command center, located in Houston, that they had landed the special lunar module safely on the moon's surface. He said, "Houston...the *Eagle* has landed." The very first word ever spoken on the moon was "Houston!" That, say Houston citizens, is something no other city can ever top.

Houston's skyline reaches toward the future.

HOUSTON THEN AND NOW

Houston today is an ultramodern city, a hub of world trade and industry. It is the site of multimillion-dollar department stores and shops. There are many interesting things to see and do. It is hard to imagine how very different Houston was a little more than 150 years ago, in 1836. The "city" was no more than a rough settlement. No one then could dream of what tiny Houston would become.

Years before Texas became a state, it was part of the land controlled by Mexico. For a while Mexico allowed Americans to come to Texas and settle there. So many settlers came to Texas, in fact, that the Mexican government got a little nervous in 1830 and stopped allowing the settlers in. The anger and resentment the Texas settlers felt erupted soon after, when the dictator Santa Anna forced his way to power in Mexico. Banding together under such leaders as Davy Crockett, Jim Bowie, and Sam Houston, the Texans fought against the Mexican army to achieve their independence.

The most famous battle, of course, took place in 1836 at the Alamo, a mission in San Antonio. The Texans lost the battle of the Alamo, but only six weeks later they had another chance to fight against the strong Mexican army. Led by Sam Houston, the Texans captured Santa Anna in the little town of San Jacinto. In exchange for Santa Anna's release, the Mexicans agreed to grant Texas its freedom.

The Allen Brothers' Land Scheme

Just a few months after the Texas army's victory, two brothers from New York decided to try to make a

Samuel Houston, whose statue stands in Hermann Park, was the first president of the Republic of Texas.

Sam Houston Park is named for the Texas hero who captured the Mexican general Antonio de Santa Anna in San Jacinto in April 1836.

fortune in real estate. John and Augustus Allen pooled their money and bought 6,642 acres of land not far from San Jacinto. The land was priced at $1.40 per acre. (As a clue to how well the Allens did, we know that the same land now is worth well over $50,000 per acre!)

The land they purchased was about 18 miles north of the battle site, near the Buffalo Bayou. A bayou is a shallow, marshy body of water connected to a lake or river. The Allens found that although their land was 50 miles inland, the Buffalo Bayou did wind its way to the Gulf of Mexico. Naming their new town Houston, after the current hero of Texas, was a good first step.

The Allen brothers wasted no time in advertising their glorious new "city" to people back in the States. They stretched the truth more than a little bit. They told people interested

A small church stands in Sam Houston Park.

Early settlers in the Houston area sometimes were surprised to find bayous such as the Armand Bayou. A bayou is a shallow, marshy body of water connected to a lake or river.

in buying lots in Houston that the city was "situated at the head of navigation, on the west bank of Buffalo Bayou." They gave people the impression that any ship could sail right into Houston along the bayou. It was never mentioned that the bayou was far too narrow and shallow for a seagoing vessel to navigate.

The advertisements worked, however. More and more people were coming from the States to settle in this new territory. Although many people were surprised by the swampy bayou, most decided to stay on. Houston even served as the capital of the Republic of Texas for a few years, until Austin became the final choice in 1839.

Access to the Sea

The people of Houston knew that the bayou was a key to their progress as a thriving city. Although it wasn't navigable to large ocean ships, barges and small steamships could get around on it. Cargo was transferred from large ships at the port of Galveston to these smaller boats and brought into Houston.

This system worked the other way, too. Crops such as cotton, grown quite abundantly in Texas, were shipped to Houston to be shaped into bales. The bales were then loaded into steamships and sent down the bayou to Galveston, where they were loaded into large ships heading all around the world. Houston, although not a true seaport, was growing nonetheless.

Beginning in the 1840's, Houstonians started the process of widening the bayou. They dredged the bottom until it was deep enough for a large ship, and widened it as best they could. The little Buffalo Bayou became the Houston Ship Channel. By 1914 Houston was officially a seaport, and today it is the nation's third busiest, after New York and New Orleans. Not bad for a town that is more than 50 miles from the sea!

Growing Up

Besides the channel, there were other reasons for the incredible growth of Houston.

The first was a tragedy at Galveston in 1900. A hurricane struck there and severely damaged what was then the busiest seaport in Texas. Thousands of people were killed, and the city was slow to recover.

Houston is a major seaport of the South.

The battleship Texas *is one of many ships named for a U.S. state.*

Houston was in a perfect position to take over the shipping business in the area.

Another reason for Houston's growth through the 20th century began in 1901. An oil well, known as Spindletop, blew—another way of saying that a fountain of oil gushed to the surface of a well—about 80 miles from Houston. Not long afterwards, another well blew, and then another. Soon it was apparent that the oil boom had begun, and Houston was right in the middle of it.

Several oil companies built refineries in Houston. The city was

The San Jacinto Monument and the battleship Texas *are Houston landmarks.*

growing at an incredible rate. More and more workers streamed into the city—workers from the oil fields, laborers who would lay miles of pipeline from the oil fields to the refineries, and business people to run the plants. Too, carpenters were needed to build homes, and additional city workers were needed for the expanding population. It seemed as though there would be no end to Houston's growth. As it nudged out Philadelphia and Detroit to be the fourth largest city in America, Houston seemed to be, in the early 1980's, unstoppable.

Houston's green grass and shrubs provide a soft contrast to the sharp lines of the city's skyline.

INSIDE HOUSTON

One first-time visitor to Houston was astonished at how much sky there was. The sky does seem to go on forever around Houston. That's because, unlike so much of the rest of Texas, the Houston area is level. Only 40 feet above sea level, the countryside is as flat as a pancake. Kids in Houston think it's great not to need more than one gear on their bikes!

Another thing that surprises visitors is the climate. Most of us think of Texas as a dry desert, but that isn't the case in Houston. Houston is noted for its unpleasant humidity. In the summer the weather is sticky and hot—about 90 degrees and humid. Winters are sticky and cool—about 45 degrees and humid.

Believe it or not, the uncomfortable humidity has played an important role in the layout of the city! Almost all of the large office com-plexes downtown are connected by a series of tunnels. That way, those who work and shop in the city can do so in air-conditioned comfort.

One native Houstonian joked that he couldn't remember ever taking a breath of real air. "Like everybody else, I have an air-conditioned home. I drive to work in my air-conditioned car, and park in an air-conditioned garage. I work, eat, and shop in nice cool air. At five o'clock I get back in my car and go home. I don't think my lungs would know what to do if they ever met up with a breath of real Houston air!"

The Layout of Houston

Houston and its suburbs have grown very fast since the comple-tion of the channel and the oil boom. Houston's population today is about

1.7 million people, and the metropolitan area has a population of more than 3 million. The majority of people are white—about 60 percent. (This 60 percent includes Mexican Americans, as well.) Nearly 35 percent of Houstonians are black. The remaining five percent are Vietnamese, Korean, or Middle Eastern.

Houston is cut, from west to east, by the Buffalo Bayou, which becomes the Houston Ship Channel at the extreme eastern end of the city. The downtown area of Houston is encircled by a loop of freeway called 610. Within that loop are the tall skyscrapers (many of them owned by various oil companies) for which Houston has become well known. Unlike cities such as Chicago and New York, where you can see a hodgepodge of the old and new, Houston is very modern. There haven't been a lot of old buildings saved. Most of the downtown buildings were built in the 1960's, '70's, and '80's.

Houston has two airports. Hous-

The fountain at Tranquility Park is a cool spot in downtown Houston. Summer weather is sticky and hot.

Most of Houston's modern downtown buildings were constructed in the 1960's, '70's, and '80's.

ton Intercontinental is about 15 miles north of downtown, while W.P. Hobby Airport is 9 miles southeast. More than 25 airlines fly in and out of Houston every day.

Pennzoil Place is one of the many oil company headquarters found in Houston. Its twin towers are only 10 feet apart, and are a recognizable part of the Houston skyline. At 75 stories, the Texas Commerce Tower is the world's tallest tube-shaped tower. Many of these modern skyscrapers have colorful sculptures and murals decorating them inside and out.

Again, because of Houston's growth, the demand for office space in Houston has grown with amazing speed in the last decade. City planners say that office space in the downtown area has doubled in the last ten years!

Also within the downtown area are many shops and department stores. Houstonians are particularly proud of Neiman-Marcus (a product of Texas), a store where you can purchase, among other things, "His and Hers" hot air balloons, a bathtub full of diamonds, or a dollhouse exactly like your own home, right down to the clothes in the closets! Many of these "specialty items" cost half a million dollars or more, and it's hard to believe that people actually purchase them!

Houston's Poor

As with any large city, Houston has its poor people. Many of Houston's poor are unemployed, and live in ugly, run-down housing. As is often the case, many of the poor are black or Mexican. The poor in Houston live near the smelly banks of the Houston Ship Channel. The southeast side of the city is a poor black area; the poor Mexican neighborhoods are east and northeast of the downtown area.

Much of the problem with poverty in Houston has to do with the thousands of Mexicans who have crossed over the border illegally. Most have come to the United States in search of a job and a better place to live. Unfortunately, many don't find work and end up in the poor neighborhoods, making crowded areas even more crowded. No one is quite sure exactly how many illegal immigrants there are in Houston, but city officials guess the current figure is about a half million. To make matters worse, they also guess that the figure is growing at the rate of 1,000 people per week!

Not all minority group members are poor, and it would be wrong to suggest that. Houston brags of the wealthiest black suburb in the nation, called MacGregor Park. MacGregor Park was originally a Jewish neighborhood. In the early part of this century Jews weren't allowed to live in some of the fashionable suburbs, so they built their own. Now, however, many of the huge homes are owned by upper-middle-class black families.

Besides Neighborhoods

Houston is unique among most American cities because it has almost no zoning laws. Zoning laws are regulations which, for example, prohibit a company from building a factory in a residential neighborhood. Most cities have zoning laws to protect homeowners from living next to businesses and high-traffic areas.

In Houston, however, there may be a bar next to a library, or a warehouse near a home! The rapid growth of Houston, both in terms of people and buildings, has made zoning plans almost impossible to make and enforce.

Besides neighborhood and business areas, Houston is also home to several colleges. Rice University, Texas Southern University, and the University of Houston are three of the 28 colleges and professional schools in Houston.

Visitors to Rice University notice that it looks a lot like an eastern Ivy League school like Yale or Harvard—except for its football stadium, that is. Houston really supports its college football teams, and you can see that firsthand. Although Rice University has a student body of about 4,000, its football stadium seats 72,000. That's more than most NFL stadiums can hold!

The Galleria gives Houstonians an opportunity to shop in cool comfort, away from the hot, humid air outside.

THE MAIN ATTRACTIONS

The Astrodomain

There are plenty of fun things to see and do around the city. Some cost money, while others are absolutely free.

One attraction near the south end of the city's freeway loop is called Astrodomain. Astrodomain is a recreational park with three main parts. The first is called the Astrohall Exhibition Center. That's a large arena where Houston's biggest event, the Houston Livestock Show and Rodeo, is held every February. For two solid weeks, the whole town dresses in cowboy attire. There are parades, concerts, rodeo events, and competitions to determine who's raised the finest horses and cattle in the state.

The second part of the center is the Astroworld Amusement Park. With more than 100 rides, As-troworld features one of the world's best (and scariest) roller coasters.

The third, and most famous, part of the Astrodomain complex is the Houston Astrodome. The Astrodome was the first enclosed—and air-conditioned—football and baseball stadium. The Houston Astros of baseball's National League, as well as the Houston Oilers of the National Football League, play all their home games here.

The Astrodome towers 19 stories above Houston. Colorful rows of black, red, gold, orange, blue, and purple seats—more than 52,000 of them—make the place look like anything but a sports facility.

When the Astrodome first opened its doors on April 9, 1965, people were astounded. Games such as football and baseball had always seemed dependent on weather. It never before had seemed possible to

The Houston Astrodome was the first baseball and football stadium with a roof. Spectators watch games in air-conditioned comfort regardless of the weather.

watch baseball and football in air-conditioned comfort. Yet there the fans sat, happily enjoying the 74-degree weather while outside the hot steamy sunshine made everything swelter. So much electricity is used at the Astrodome, it is said, that the powerful system could light a town of over 9,000 people! But the fact that the place was air-conditioned was only the beginning.

A $2 million scoreboard made the games more "show biz" than just sports. The scoreboard is longer than the football field; several skilled people are needed to operate it. Sunlight streamed in from 4,600 plastic skylights, providing the light needed for spectators and players. Unfortunately, there was *not* enough light, or the right kind of light, to keep the grass growing. And you couldn't play football or baseball without grass, right?

Wrong—at least as far as Houston was concerned. To solve the problem of what to play on, Astroturf was invented. Astroturf is the green-colored carpet that masquerades as grass in the Astrodome and other domed stadiums that have sprung up around the country.

Astroturf is not as soft and springy as grass. For baseball, players wear regular cleats, since there is dirt in the infield. But for football, soccer shoes are the best footwear. Most football players don't like it much, since it leads to more injuries than does real grass. Major league pitchers don't care for it because baseballs bounce on it, often turning an easy grounder to the infield into a base hit. But, as one Houstonian observed, the stuff has one big advantage—you don't need to water it.

The Houston Astros of baseball's National League and the Houston Oilers of the National Football League play all their home games in the Astrodome.

Plenty of Parks in Houston

There are 270 parks in and around Houston. Hermann Park covers 545 acres of southwest Houston, and has more things to do than you could imagine!

There is a planetarium at Hermann Park, as well as a free zoo. In fact, Houstonians are proud that their city has one of the last free zoos in the whole country. Without a doubt, the most popular animal exhibit there is an albino diamondback rattlesnake with pink eyes. Those who study reptiles say that such a snake is extremely rare.

Hermann Park also has a huge rose garden, and a special fragrance garden for blind people. There are acres and acres of beautiful woods, and a little train just for kids runs through the park.

In the summer the famous Houston Symphony gives free concerts at the Miller Outdoor Theatre that lies on the fringe of Hermann Park.

The Houston Symphony gives free summer concerts at the Miller Outdoor Theatre in Hermann Park.

The Wortham Theatre Center contributes to Houston's cultural activities.

San Jacinto State Park is located about 20 miles from downtown, to the east. It was here that Sam Houston and his band of Texas rebels fought the 18-minute battle over 150 years ago that won Texas' independence from Mexico. A 570-foot-high monument at San Jacinto tells the whole story of the battle. Unfortunately, because the land is so marshy, the monument continues to sink, and the area around it is sometimes closed for repair.

The 570-foot-high San Jacinto Monument tells the story of Sam Houston's successful battle for Texas' independence from Mexico.

The Museum of Fine Arts has a collection of art and antiques once owned by Ima Hogg. The museum also has a collection of artwork from Egypt and Greece.

The First Lady of Houston Art

Many people who visit Houston enjoy touring the mansion of Ima Hogg, the daughter of former governor James Hogg. She was one of the most famous collectors of antiques in the entire country, and today her collection is part of the Museum of Fine Arts in Houston.

The mansion is called Bayou Bend, and in it there are samples of furniture, crafts, and other collectors' items from the 1600's through the 1890's not found anywhere else in Texas, or, for that matter, the United States. Before Miss Ima died at the age of 83, she bequeathed the mansion, where she had lived for 40 years, to the Houston museum.

And, contrary to that old Texas joke, Miss Ima did **not** have a sister named Ura!

For Higher Tastes

The Lyndon Baines Johnson Space Center, located 20 miles southeast of the downtown area, is another fascinating place to visit. The Center is spread out over more than 1600 acres, and is made up of 100 different buildings, only five of which are open to the public.

The Space Center is the command post for every manned U.S. space flight. It is also the training center for all men and women who have been chosen to become astronauts. There are spacecraft displays, training simulators, and a movie about the space program.

A visit to the Houston Grand Opera is another activity for people with "high tastes." The opera company has a great reputation for performing old and new works, and they also feature internationally known guest singers. What makes the Houston Grand Opera a little bit different is that the people who manage it seem to understand that many opera goers don't know much Italian and German—two of the most common languages for classic opera. To make it easier on those people, there is a computerized translation of what you hear on stage, printed out above the arch of the stage!

The Lyndon B. Johnson Space Center, named for the 36th president of the United States, covers 1,600 acres.

INDUSTRY & TRADE

Oil is King

Several industries are important to the economy of Houston, but the most important is oil. No less than 30 major oil companies have their headquarters in Houston.

Sometimes people forget that oil is not just important to make gasoline for cars and trucks, although that certainly is where a lot of oil goes. Oil is also important because of its by-products. By-products are the results of changing the oil, either by heating it or changing it chemically.

The production of certain by-products from crude oil and natural gas, called petrochemicals, is big business. Petrochemicals with such hard-to-spell names as benzine, ethylene, and propylene are produced in great abundance in Houston. Fertilizers, insecticides, and ink for newspapers—all are made from petrochemicals, and all are produced in large factories along the Houston Ship Channel. Synthetic or artificial rubber is produced from petrochemicals, too—in fact, 80 percent of all the rubber made in the United States is made in Houston!

All of the factories, oil refineries, and petrochemical plants line the Houston Ship Channel. Beneath them all lies a maze of pipeline—over 1,000 miles of it—carrying chemicals and oil by-products. This jumble of pipes is referred to as the "Spaghetti Bowl."

The Key to Houston's Trade

Without a doubt, Houston wouldn't be nearly as important if it weren't for its link with the sea—the Houston Ship Channel. Because of it Houston is the Southwest's leading trade center. Ships and sailors from all over the world come to Houston. The international feeling of Houston is evident in the kind of goods it has for sale, the languages that can be heard on the streets, and even the many types of restaurants in Houston.

The channel was completed in 1914, but those who depend on the channel know that it never will be

Oil production and shipping are important parts of Houston's economy.

truly completed. The channel needs to be dredged out every year because of all the settling of mud and silt. It must be kept at least 40 feet deep for the huge seagoing ships to safely use it. The cost of the dredging is more than $7 million per year, but Houstonians know it's worth it. The channel accounts for over $18 billion in foreign trade yearly. Besides, there are 32,000 jobs in Houston that depend on the channel—from dock workers to the Coast Guard personnel who monitor the ships.

Every day of the year, 24 hours per day, the channel is busy. There are remote-controlled video cameras set up at certain corners so channel workers can make sure of the whereabouts of each ship. The channel is so curvy and crooked that without close supervision by the Coast Guard, ships could collide. Because of the explosive contents of most of these ships, such an event would be a catastrophe.

The Houston Ship Channel, dug in 1914, connects the city to Galveston Bay and then the Gulf of Mexico. The channel begins at Buffalo Bayou.

The Business of Medicine

Houston is also famous for its Texas Medical Center, a 235-acre complex located in the south part of the city. The Center treats between 1.5 and 2 million people every year.

Two of the world's most renowned heart surgeons, Dr. Michael Debakey and Dr. Denton Cooley, operate at the Center. Dr. Debakey is known as the "Miracle Man of Medicine." Together with a team of surgeons and technicians from Rice University and the Baylor University College of Medicine, Debakey created the first artificial heart.

The Center is not one hospital, but nine. There are also four medical and nursing schools and several research institutions. Although all of the hospitals are excellent, the most famous one is the M.D. Anderson Hospital and Tumor Institute. The Anderson Hospital specializes in the care and aggressive treatment of many kinds of cancers.

The medical staff at the Texas Medical Center, a 235-acre complex, treats nearly two million people each year.

GOVERNING THE PEOPLE

Houston has a "strong mayor" form of government. That means that the mayor has more power than any group of city-wide representatives, such as a city council.

Houston citizens elect the mayor and fourteen council representatives for two-year terms. The mayor appoints the department heads in the city, such as the fire chief and the

The Brown Convention Center offers Texas hospitality to convention goers and other large groups of people.

chief of police. The only administrator not appointed by the mayor is the city controller.

There is no city manager; the mayor does most of the decision-making for the city, and presides over all the meetings of the city council. At these meetings, the city council must then decide whether to support or reject the mayor's proposals.

For the first time in its history, the city of Houston has a woman mayor. Her name is Kathy Whitmire, and she has a large following among Houstonians. Mayor Whitmire feels that there are a lot of challenges in leading a city like Houston.

For instance, because there are no zoning laws in Houston, a good mayor must keep up with all current building going on at any given time. Since the city has no built-in regulations, the mayor and the council must use good sense in what kinds of businesses are built where. She likes the fact that there is lots of freedom in Houston's government so that she can appoint, reject, and decide things that she feels are in the city's best interest.

Houston's many fountains, such as this one at Bayou Bend, are a refreshing sight to both visitors and natives.

FINDING A BETTER WAY

The years between 1970 and 1980 were the peak of Houston's growth. Downtown business building and the building of new homes in residential areas skyrocketed. Everybody was hiring workers to build, to expand, to grow. Because oil was so very important to our nation, the key to Houston's explosion seemed to be the refining and production of oil.

In this way, Houston seemed to fall into a sort of "boomtown" trap. A boomtown is one that springs up and grows very quickly because a discovery such as gold or oil is made nearby. Lots of people flock to the town, and things seem to be prosperous and promising. But when the gold is all mined, or the oil wells dry up, lots of boomtowns turn into ghost towns. Without the hope of making their fortunes, many people move away.

Houston prospered even more during the world-wide oil shortages in the late 1970's and early '80's. Because the U.S. wasn't getting oil from the Middle East, Texas oil was even more valuable. The price of a barrel of oil rose, and Houstonians were excited. Business boomed. The city expanded as fast as the money rolled in.

But as the oil shortage subsided in the mid-80's, the price of oil dropped. Companies that staked their whole bankroll on a booming economy fell by the wayside. As a result, real estate all over the city dropped in price. People not only weren't building new houses, many of those people weren't working at all. In 1983, for instance, 100,000 jobs were lost. CBS News reported that Houston had more unoccupied office space than either Denver or San Francisco had in total office space!

Such unemployment led to pov-

The Transco Tower fountain is a Houston landmark, and a symbol of better times.

erty, and poverty seemed to lead to overcrowding and more crime. Racial tensions also increased. Houston had always been controlled by white conservative politicians, and the city's black and Mexican-American people felt that they weren't being listened to enough.

To make matters worse, some of the things that never seemed to get done as the city was booming, such as fixing the city's poor highway system and modernizing the sewage treatment facilities, were now almost impossible to think about. Houstonians felt that the city should have done those things when the money was there.

Houston has been plagued by many transportation problems. Many of the roads are in need of repair. There are many two-lane roads that are simply not adequate for the amount of traffic they receive. Citizens have been asking for years for more freeways to relieve the slow, stop-and-go roads.

In addition to the poor roads, Houston has no reliable public transportation system. Although there have been proposals for commuter rail service and ultra-fast buses, no real progress has been made as yet. As one city official said, "Houston has grown too fast. In the past, any transportation the city would have built would have taken several years to complete. By the time it would have been completed, Houston's exploding population would have made it instantly obsolete!"

Because of hard work and good city government, Houston is in a little more stable position these days. Things certainly aren't booming, but people are being more realistic about their money. Mayor Whitmire is trying to broaden the economy, to not depend so much on oil production. Instead, she wants to concentrate on the medical industry and the space program, two very important aspects of Houston's economy. Houston wants to improve its public transportation, although everyone agrees that progress will take time.

One of the first things Mayor Whitmire did was to appoint Lee Brown, a black man, as chief of police. That seemed to send a mes-

Downtown Houston lights up the night sky.

sage to the black community that Houston was ready to make some changes. Having had strong backing in her mayoral race from Mexican-Americans and blacks, the mayor realizes that Houston needs to listen more carefully to the needs of its poor. To become a stable and progressive city into the 21st century, Houston needs the help and energy of all its citizens.

*Houston, Texas

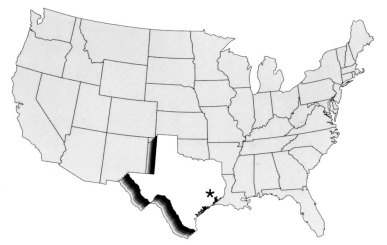

IMPORTANT FACTS

- Population: 1,730,000 (1988 estimate)
  Rank: 4
- Population of metropolitan area: 3,230,700
- Mayor: Kathryn Whitmire (next election, December 1989)
- Seat of Harris County

- Land area: 579,58 sq. miles
- Monthly normal temperature:
  January—51.4°F
  July—83.1°F
- Average annual precipitation: 44.76"
- Latitude: 29° 45' 26" N
- Longitude: 95° 21' 37" W
- Altitude: ranges from sea level to 120 ft.

- Time zone: Central

- Annual events:
  Houston Livestock Show, Parade & Rodeo, Astrodome, March
  Houston International Festival, April
  Houston Anniversary Celebration, August
  Greek Festival, October
  Candlelight Tours, Sam Houston Park, December
  Bluebonnet Bowl, December 31

IMPORTANT DATES

1830—Texas area controlled by Mexico.

1836—Texas settlers defeated by Mexico in Battle of the Alamo; later, Texans captured Mexican leader Santa Anna in town of San Jacinto and successfully bargained for Texas' freedom.

1836—Allen brothers bought land in Texas; named settlement Houston. Many settlers moved to area.

1837—Houston incorporated as city.

1840's—Houstonians began widening bayou, which became Houston Ship Channel.

1900—hurricane in Galveston damaged that seaport; Houston expanded its position as seaport.

1901—oil well "Spindletop" blew near Houston; start of oil boom.

1965—official opening of the Astrodome.

1969—Johnson Space Center in Houston was command post for first landing on the moon.

late 1970's-early '80's—worldwide oil shortage raised oil prices; Houston prospered and its population grew quickly.

1983—oil prices dropped; Houston's economy suffered; unemployment became a serious problem.

mid-1980's—Houston slowly recovered.

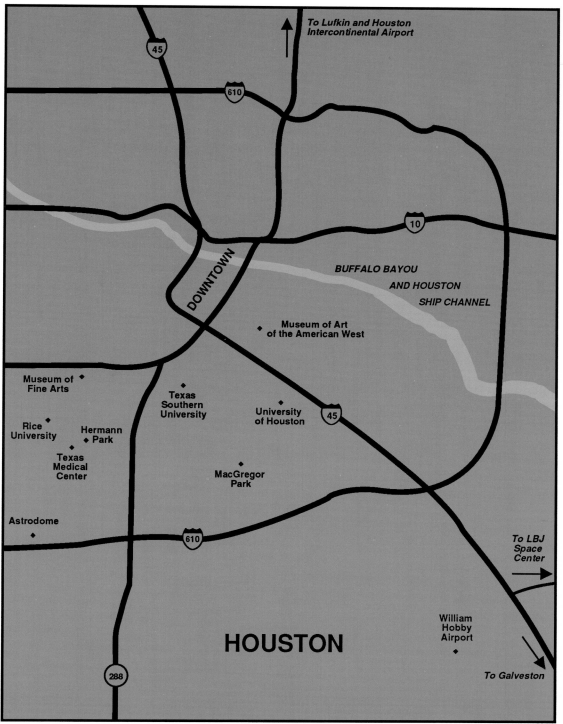

To Lufkin and Houston
Intercontinental Airport

DOWNTOWN

BUFFALO BAYOU
AND HOUSTON
SHIP CHANNEL

Museum of Art
of the American West

Museum of
Fine Arts

Texas
Southern
University

University
of Houston

Rice
University

Hermann
Park

Texas
Medical
Center

MacGregor
Park

Astrodome

To LBJ
Space
Center

William
Hobby
Airport

HOUSTON

To Galveston

©1989 Mark E. Ahlstrom

★ GLOSSARY ★

Allen, Augustus and John—brothers who invested in land (now Houston) after Texas won independence from Mexico.

Astrodomain—a recreational park near downtown Houston.

Astrodome—the world's first domed football/baseball stadium.

Astroturf—fake "grass" used in the Astrodome.

bayou—a shallow, swampy part of a river.

boomtown—a town in history that springs up because of a sudden discovery, such as oil or gold. Boomtowns often grow too quickly and end up being ghost towns!

by-product—something that is made from something else.

crude oil—the natural state of oil before it is cleaned and changed by heat or chemicals.

Galveston—a large seaport near Houston. Formerly the largest seaport in Texas before a hurricane destroyed the town.

Hogg, Ima—the "first lady" of Texas art and antiques.

Houston, Sam—the leader in Texas' fight for independence.

Houston Ship Channel—the winding body of water that connects Houston to the Gulf of Mexico, 50 miles away. The channel enables Houston to be an international port.

MacGregor Park—the wealthiest black suburb in the U.S., located in Houston.

petrochemicals—by-products of oil or natural gas.

refine—to clean or make pure.

Santa Anna—the Mexican dictator who fought against Sam Houston in Texas' struggle for independence.

San Jacinto—the site of Sam Houston's victory over the Mexican army of Santa Anna.

Spaghetti Bowl—the network of pipes connecting all of the factories and chemical plants along the Houston Ship Channel.

Spindletop—an oil well 80 miles from Houston that "blew" in 1901. That event began the oil boom in Texas.

synthetic—made by people.

zoning laws—rules that state what sort of businesses are allowed in residential neighborhoods.

INDEX